WINNING
YOUR WORLD

BECOMING THE PERSON OF INFLUENCE
GOD CREATED YOU TO BE

MAC HAMMOND

Winning Your World—
Becoming the Person of Influence God Created You to Be
ISBN 978-1-57399-102-5
© 2000, 2006, 2018 by Mac Hammond
Published by Mac Hammond Ministries
PO Box 29469
Minneapolis, MN 55429

TABLE OF CONTENTS

INTRODUCTION

Witnessing. Testifying. Evangelism. Just the words are enough to tie knots in the stomach of many a believer. In fact, nothing in the Christian life is more likely to induce knocking knees, stammering lips, and nervous perspiration than the prospect of trying to influence an unsaved person with the Gospel.

To the majority of believers, evangelism means risking confrontation, inviting rejection, and suffering embarrassment. With that kind of image firmly entrenched in our minds, it's no wonder more of us aren't seeking to influence others for Jesus. But is this frightful image an accurate one?

The wonderful answer to that question is "no." The Lord never intended evangelism to be a fearsome, dreaded chore. On the contrary, true evangelism is something that can and should flow naturally out of your relationship with Jesus Christ. In fact, it is possible to adopt a style of evangelism that is custom tailored to your own individual personality, temperament, and giftings.

Helping you discover the style of evangelism that is perfect for you is what this book is all about. In the process, you'll also learn how to cultivate a desire to be involved in evangelism. Rather than being guilt-tripped or shamed into telling others about Jesus, you'll *want* to do it.

Once you understand the principles described in the following pages, you'll never think of evangelism in the same way again. So get ready to discover the joy of becoming the person of influence God created you to be!

Mac Hammond

Chapter 1

WHY EVANGELIZE?

"What's in it for me?" It's a question even most selfless Christians asks themselves from time to time. It's a self-centered concern, no doubt. But as long as we're trapped in this corruptible body of flesh, it's one all of us are bound to ask.

So when it comes to the issue of evangelism, don't be shocked if you find yourself wondering, *Why should I expend great effort and time in evangelism when I have so many personal needs in my own life?* The fact is, there is something for you to gain. I can sum it up in one word—power. The power to change your circumstances.

Evangelism releases the power of God in your life in a way few other activities can. Why is that? Because God doesn't indiscriminately bestow His power upon us. He releases it to those who align themselves with His purposes. And God's overriding purpose in the earth in this age is to bring people back into fellowship with Himself.

Let's be honest. If there is anything the body of Christ needs right now, it's an infusion of Holy Spirit power. Far too many believers are living lives characterized by powerlessness. We seem helpless to substantially affect our own circumstances, much less those of a hurting, dying world. I believe the reason for this lack of power is that we have failed to align ourselves with God's purposes.

THREE KINDS OF POWER

God has made three basic arenas of power available to us to make us effective evangelists. The first is found in Ephesians 1:18–19. Here Paul prays for his readers:

> *The eyes of your understanding being enlightened; that you may know what is the hope of His calling, what are the riches of the glory of His inheritance in the saints, and what is the exceeding greatness of His power toward us who believe, according to the working of His mighty power.*

To whom is this power directed? To those of us "who believe." This power is the power of faith. It's available to every Christian and is the same power that raised Jesus from the dead. In other words, it's an awesome, unlimited power source.

Why did He give that power to us? According to the verse above, so that we might fulfill His call upon our lives ("the hope of His calling") and become His richly glorious inheritance ("His inheritance in the saints").

Yes, we are to be the glorious inheritance of God Himself. And I don't have to tell you, it's not glorious to be sick. It's not glorious to be plagued by lack and insufficiency. It's not glorious to live under a dark cloud of oppression. God receives no glory when your relationships are characterized by strife.

That's what that mighty "toward us" power Paul talks about is for—to drive those things out of your life. Then and only then will your life be a glorious inheritance for God.

"But, Mac, why would God want me for a glorious inheritance?"

First and foremost because He loves you. But just as importantly, so you will be a light to a lost world. When the world sees the power of God transforming your life, ridding your body of sickness, bringing prosperity to your household and restoring your marriage, it will shine like a beacon in this dark time in which we live.

This is the first type of power God wants to release in our lives as we align with His plans and purposes—particularly His plan to redeem fallen men and women. It's the power of faith.

HOLY SPIRIT POWER

The second kind of power available to the believer is the power of the Holy Spirit. This type of power includes the gifts of the Spirit such as the working of miracles, special faith, and gifts of healing. The promise of this power is given by Jesus Himself in Acts 1:8:

But you shall receive power when the Holy Spirit has come upon you; and you shall be witnesses to Me in Jerusalem, and in all Judea and Samaria, and to the end of the earth.

The Greek word translated power in this verse is *dunamis*, which refers to miracle-working power. The Holy Spirit comes upon you to bring power into your life. For what purpose? To make you an effective evangelist. Once again, we see that power comes as we align our lives with God's purposes.

THE POWER OF DOMINION

The third type of power available to the believer is the power of dominion and authority. Jesus spoke about it in Matthew 28:18–19:

> *And Jesus came and spoke to them, saying, "All authority has been given to Me in heaven and on earth. Go therefore and make disciples of all the nations, baptizing them in the name of the Father and of the Son and of the Holy Spirit...."*

This is an extraordinary passage of scripture. Jesus first declares that all authority (*exousia*—authority, dominion, jurisdiction) in heaven and on earth has been given to Him. Then He delegates that supreme authority to all believers who follow His commission to take the Gospel into all the world. That's you and me.

In the name of Jesus, we can cause demons to bow their knees, we can cast out devils, we can lay hands on the sick and see them recover. In that name that is above every name, we have power (authority, dominion, and jurisdiction) over everything the enemy can bring our way.

Why are we given such enormous authority? So we may "Go ye therefore, and teach all nations." In other words, we're to use our Christ-given dominion to spread the Gospel.

All three types of power—the power of faith, the power of the Holy Spirit, and the power of authority—are given to the believer to equip him or her to be an effective evangelist. If you want heaven's power operating on your behalf to keep you prosperous, healthy, and peaceful, then get your life in line with God's purpose for that power. Get involved in influencing others with the Gospel of Jesus Christ. That's what's in it for you.

This isn't a hard concept to grasp. The Bible makes it very clear. Yet, it's one of the hardest to communicate to some people. The message is simple. If you want your inner problems solved, turn your attention outward. Get your attention off your needs and onto someone else's needs.

Job is a great example of this principle in operation. For 40 chapters, Job moaned and groaned to God, his wife, his friends, and anyone else who would listen. Yet his circumstance didn't change. Then at God's prompting, he prayed for his friends. He turned his attention and intercession outward. You know the result. Immediately, his situation began to turn around.

If you want the power of God operating in your life, you're going to have to align yourself with His most basic of purposes— letting a lost and dying world know that there is life, rest, peace, and wholeness in Jesus Christ.

Chapter 2

STAYING MOTIVATED
FOR EVANGELISM

"Okay, Mac, you've convinced me. I want the power of God to be released in my life, so I'm going to line up with God's purposes and start seeing opportunities to evangelize others."

Good. You're motivated, for now anyway. But what happens to your newfound zeal the first time you come up against some real persecution? If you're like many believers, it will simply wither like a flower in the scorching desert sun.

It is vital that you, as a Christian dedicated to influencing others with the Gospel, know how to maintain your motivation in the face of persecution. And I can assure you, if you're truly living your faith, you *will* experience persecution. If you've never experienced it, you're either a closet Christian or you've never been born again at all.

Persecution and rejection are simply a part of the committed Christian's life. (2 Timothy 3:12) That's because there's a Devil out there and he still has people in the world who allow him to work through them.

So how do you keep yourself motivated to a point that your desire to exert godly influence with others is greater than your concern about persecution and rejection? There are several scriptural keys.

First, you must realize you are designed to have a desire for the things, good or bad, to which you give your attention. In other words, pay enough attention to something and you are going to have a desire for that thing. This holds true for everything from chocolate cake to pornography. It's also true for the things of God.

If you'll give attention to the things God's Word says about being an ambassador for Christ, you'll begin cultivating a desire to be one. Don't allow things in the world to capture your attention—your focus. Ungodly desire is the sure result. Direct your focus (thought life, meditation, attention) to the mandate of Scripture, and the desire to influence others with the Gospel will arise.

In addition to such disciplined management of your focus, ask God for these specific heart revelations.

A PLACE CALLED HELL

The first revelation you need to stay motivated in the face of persecution is a revelation of hell. When the horrifying reality of hell sinks in, you can't help focusing on others and seeking to consistently influence them with the Gospel. We see this principle in operation in a true story Jesus once told His listeners.

In Luke 16:19–31, Jesus tells us of a rich man who had no time for the things of God during his life. But when he died and got a glimpse of hell, he suddenly became very evangelistic. He pleaded with Abraham to send a beggar named Lazarus to warn his family about the awfulness of hell:

Then he said, "I beg you therefore, father, that you would send him to my father's house, for I have five brothers, that he may testify to them, lest they also come to this place of torment." (Luke 16:27–28)

This isn't some fairy tale. It's a grim glimpse, delivered by the Son of God Himself, of what lies on the other side of the veil we call death. It's called hell, and it wasn't meant for you or any other person. It's a place prepared for Satan and his angels. Yet, it is the ultimate destination for any person who aligns himself with the satanic rebellion by rejecting Jesus Christ.

The good news is, you can use this truth to stay focused on the need to evangelize. A true revelation of hell, however, simply cannot be imparted intellectually. It is something God must reveal to you on a spiritual level.

I vividly remember when God opened my eyes to the reality of hell. Prior to that time, hell had been more of a vague concept to me than a genuine place. As a result, I had been asking God to make hell real to me. I knew I needed that revelation if I were to have the proper motivation to do things I knew I should do.

The answer came in the form of a vision. I saw a countless multitude being pushed toward the edge of a cliff. At the bottom of that cliff was hell. Rising up from the abyss, I heard the most awful screams and wails I'd ever heard.

The river of humanity endlessly flowed toward the edge, the people at the back having no idea what lay ahead. Then my attention was drawn to a father who was leading his little girl by the hand. His facial expression was that of a man who was trying not to show how frightened he was. He obviously didn't know where he was going. He was just following the crowd.

Ever so often his little girl would look up at him with a terrified look in her eyes and ask, "Daddy, is everything going to be all right?" And he says, "Yes, honey, just keep walking."

The closer the pitiful couple got to the edge, the louder the horrifying screams grew and the more frightened they became. Yet the man continued to follow the crowd and led his daughter the same way.

Hell became a real place to me that day. I've never thought about it the same way since. I know as never before—this isn't a game. The things we do now are going to determine where some people spend eternity. A revelation of hell will keep you motivated like few other things can.

JUST REWARDS

The second revelation that will help you stay motivated toward evangelism and influencing others for God is a revelation of rewards.

The Bible has quite a bit to say about the rewards (both in this life and in eternity) that await those who are obedient to Jesus' Great Commission. Look, for example, at Luke 16:9, "And I say to you, make friends for yourselves by unrighteous mammon, that when you fail, they may receive you into everlasting habitations."

The picture this verse paints is, "If you'll use your money to get people saved, when you die, they're going to be there waiting to receive you into heaven. When you go home to be with the Lord, all these people are going to be lining the pearly gates to welcome you." Peter calls it "an abundant entrance" (2 Peter 1:11).

I want an abundant entrance when I get to heaven. Don't you? I don't want to just sneak in under the wire. I want my Savior to look me in the eye and say, "Well done, good and faithful servant" (Matthew 25:21). Daniel tells us that those who have steered others into the path of righteousness in this life will be accorded special honor in eternity: "Those who are wise shall shine like the brightness of the firmament, and those who turn many to righteousness like the stars forever and ever" (Daniel 12:3).

Not only are there tremendous rewards in heaven awaiting believers who engage in evangelism, there are plenty of rewards right here and now. To me there is nothing more gratifying than to have someone I've helped find the Lord come up to me and say, "You changed my life. You changed my eternal destiny. Thank you."

I must tell you, I get overwhelmed when that happens. It's one of the greatest feelings on earth. And it's one of the many rewards, both present and future, for the believer who will risk occasional rejection in order to influence others for Jesus. Getting a revelation of those rewards is one important way to stay motivated to do just that.

THE STOCKPILE FACTOR

The third revelation you need to receive to help you maintain a desire to evangelize others is a revelation of what I call "the stockpile factor." It's a concept derived from a remarkable series of events described in 2 Kings 6:24–25:

> *And it happened after this that Ben-Hadad king of Syria gathered all his army, and went up and besieged Samaria. And there was a great famine in Samaria; and indeed they besieged it until a donkey's head was sold for eighty shekels of silver, and one-fourth of a kab of dove droppings for five shekels of silver.*

I don't have to tell you, when donkey heads and bird droppings become highly coveted grocery items, times are tough.

Samaria was experiencing a famine because Syria had the whole city surrounded. No one could get in or get out. The people inside the city were starving. That is the backdrop for what we begin reading about in 2 Kings 7:3–9:

> *Now there were four leprous men at the entrance of the gate; and they said to one another, "Why are we sitting here until we die? If we say, 'We will enter the city,' the famine is in the city, and we shall die there. And if we sit here, we die also. Now therefore, come, let us surrender to the army of the Syrians. If they keep us alive, we shall live; and if they kill us, we shall but die."*

These four lepers had a flash of brilliant insight. "What have we got to lose? Let's go see if the Syrians will feed us. The worst that can happen is they kill us, and we're dying anyway."

And they rose at twilight to go to the camp of the Syrians; and when they had come to the outskirts of the Syrian camp, to their surprise no one was there. For the Lord had caused the army of the Syrians to hear the noise of chariots and the noise of horses— the noise of a great army; so they said to one another, "Look, the king of Israel has hired against us the kings of the Hittites and the kings of the Egyptians to attack us!" Therefore they arose and fled at twilight, and left the camp intact—their tents, their horses, and their donkeys—and they fled for their lives.

God had supernaturally frightened the Syrian army into running away and leaving all their supplies behind.

And when these lepers came to the outskirts of the camp, they went into one tent and ate and drank, and carried from it silver and gold and clothing, and went and hid them; then they came back and entered another tent, and carried some from there also, and went and hid it. Then they said to one another, "We are not doing what is right. This day is a day of good news, and we remain silent. If we wait until morning light, some punishment will come upon us. Now therefore, come, let us go and tell the king's household."

Here is where this account becomes relevant to the subject of evangelism. One of the strongest motivations of all for seeking to influence others about Jesus is a realization of the abundant provision we have in Him.

Just like the people of Samaria, people all around you are literally starving. They're starving for peace. Starving for healing. Starving for forgiveness. Starving for spiritual life. Just like those lepers, you've discovered a veritable king's treasure of provision if you know Jesus Christ. "Treasure?" you ask. Yes! God is supplying all your needs according to "His riches in glory" by Christ Jesus (Philippians 4:19).

When that reality hits home, you'll respond the same way those lepers did. You'll say, "I can't keep this to myself. I must tell them, 'You don't have to starve anymore. I've discovered a wealth of provision. Come see for yourself.'"

That's why Satan works overtime to keep you focused on your own needs. Once you recognize all that is yours in Christ Jesus, you're likely to run out and tell someone else about it.

DO IT FOR LOVE

Finally, the ultimate and overriding motivation for engaging in evangelism is love. Specifically, the love of Christ.

When you love people, you care about the things they care about. You count as precious those things they hold dear. Well, Jesus cares about lost people. He shed His priceless blood to ransom them from the deadly grip of Satan. He gave His everything for the rankest, vilest sinner that ever walked the earth.

Being in love with Jesus means sharing in His love and concern for a dying world. It means seeing seemingly cold and callused individuals through His eyes—the eyes of compassion.

The love of Christ, along with clear revelations of hell, rewards, and the stockpile factor will give you all the motivation you need to proclaim your faith in the face of the harshest persecution.

Motivation alone, however, will not make you an effective evangelist. To truly be successful in winning others to Christ, you need to have a sound strategy. Read on to discover one.

Chapter 3

THE STRATEGY FOR PERSONAL EVANGELISM

Once you are properly motivated to engage in evangelism, you then need to know what kind of strategy will produce the results you desire. Simply put, you need to know what works.

As always, our model for success is Jesus Christ, the author and finisher of our faith. In any endeavor in life, following His example is sure to bring outstanding results. Did Jesus give us a prescription for success when it comes to influencing others for God? Yes! We find it in Matthew 4:18–19: "Now Jesus, walking by the Sea of Galilee, saw two brothers, Simon called Peter, and Andrew his brother, casting a net into the sea; for they were fishermen. And He said to them, 'Follow Me, and I will make you fishers of men.'"

Following Jesus invariably involves joining Him in His quest for people. Notice He didn't say, "Follow Me and I'll make you successful." He didn't say, "Follow Me and I'll make you a good businessman." No, He said, "Follow Me, and I will make you fishers of men." This is the central focus of the Christ-centered life.

Blessing and success are merely byproducts of following Jesus. They are signposts that tell you you're on the right path. If you're following Him to be a fisher of men, you'll find yourself healed. You'll find your needs met. You'll find you're successful in business. But the objective is always winning the world.

So how does this give us the key to a successful strategy for doing just that? It lies in Jesus' comparison of evangelism to fishing. It's no accident Jesus used a fishing metaphor when speaking of the call to proclaim the good news. Peter and Andrew were fishermen by trade. But the illustration is relevant to us, as well.

LEARNING TO FISH

Of course, if you're an avid angler, all of this will make a lot of sense to you. But even if you've never baited a hook in your life, you must understand how to be a successful fisherman in order to have a successful strategy in evangelism.

First, let's make a distinction between two main types of fishing. One type of fishing involves the use of nets. Professional fishermen use large nets to harvest huge numbers of fish at one time. This is the type of fishing in which we see Peter, Andrew, James, and John engaged in Luke 5.

This kind of fishing can be compared to mass evangelism. When we have a meeting and large numbers of people come forward to accept Christ, we are casting forth a net and bringing in a big harvest of people. This, however, is not the type of fishing to which Jesus was referring when He said He'd make us "fishers of men."

The type of fishing that relates to one-on-one evangelism involves the use of a line and a hook. "But, Mac, they didn't have fishing poles back in Jesus' time, did they?"

Well, they may not have had Zebco spin casters and graphite rods, but they definitely used a hook and line. Look at Matthew 17:27. It describes the occasion on which Jesus and Peter needed money to pay the temple tax. Jesus tells Peter to "...go to the sea, cast in a hook, and take the fish that comes up first. And when you have opened its mouth, you will find a piece of money; take that and give it to them for Me and you."

So you see, there was another form of fishing in Jesus' day. This type symbolizes what I call "lifestyle evangelism." It is a person-to-person, one-on-one contact that results in someone giving his heart and life to Jesus Christ.

Yes, Jesus has called you to be a fisher of men. And unless you have a special calling as an evangelist, you're going to bring them into the kingdom of God one fish at a time.

"But how?" you may ask. The answer lies in Jesus' comparison of evangelism to fishing. The same things that make for a successful day of fishing will also make for success in winning people. The following principles of good fishing are your guide to being an outstanding evangelist.

1. GO WHERE THE FISH ARE

I remember an occasion back when my sons were young in which I found them standing at the edge of a mud puddle, fishing poles in hand, waiting for the fish to bite. There was just one problem. There were no fish in the mud puddle.

To catch fish, you must go where the fish are. Today, fishermen have sophisticated sonar and depth finders that permit them to "see" the bottom of the lake and to locate schools of fish. Any fisherman worth his salt knows that to catch fish, you must first *find* fish.

The same is true when it comes to evangelism. Too often our tendency is to remain in the comfort of our church and familiar social circle of believers. As a result, we become totally isolated and separated from lost people. Then we wonder why we never have the opportunity to influence others with the Gospel.

If you're going to win people, you've got to go where the lost people are. The most natural place to evangelize is to lost relatives and friends. Regrettably, most of us alienate every lost person we know within a few weeks of being born again.

While it is important (especially for a young believer) not to maintain close, intimate fellowship with unbelievers, you shouldn't close the door on opportunities to influence them with the Gospel. Maintain relationships (not fellowship) with people in the world. It's where the fish are.

When we barricade ourselves behind the four walls of the church, we miss the entire purpose of God for our lives and rob ourselves of His enabling power to change the world around us.

2. GO WHERE THE FISH ARE HUNGRY

Any angler will tell you, it is not enough to just go where the fish are. You must go where the fish are biting. There is nothing more frustrating to a fisherman than to be sitting on top of a big school of fish that are completely uninterested in eating.

If the fish aren't biting, it doesn't matter what type of bait or lures you put on your line. You're not going to catch any fish.

This is no less true in evangelism. We experienced a prime example of this in the church I pastor. In the early years, we frequently sent evangelism teams into the neighborhoods right around the church building. To our dismay, these teams experienced very little success. Why? The fish weren't hungry.

Then, as I was praying about the situation one evening, the Lord impressed me that we weren't going where the harvest is ripe. Yes, there was a harvest around our church, but it was not yet ripe.

So, instead, we started focusing our attention on the inner city where the needs were greatest. Immediately we started seeing hundreds of individuals coming into the kingdom of God. Why? Because now we were fishing where the fish were hungry.

To be a successful evangelist, you must find the hungry fish. How? By following the direction of the Master Fisherman, Jesus. He directed Peter to go to a certain place at a certain time to catch a fish. Likewise, Jesus, through the Holy Spirit, will guide you to the right places and times to meet a person hungry for the things of God. You simply must have an open and hearing heart.

Follow the leading of the Spirit as you seek to influence others with the Gospel. Don't just blast anybody that gets in your path with your gospel shotgun. That is how many people get turned off and hardened to our message.

Learn to allow the Spirit of God to lead you to the hungry fish.

3. USE THE RIGHT BAIT

Once you've found some hungry fish, the next important key to landing them is using an appropriate bait. I've yet to meet the fisherman who was so skilled that he could throw a naked hook into the water and catch a fish. It's a simple, inescapable fact—fishermen have to use bait.

Successful lifestyle evangelism involves the use of bait as well. You are probably aware that God created each of us a three-part being— spirit, soul, and body. Now, a good bait in evangelism is something that attracts a person at either the physical or soulish level.

Why not try to attract a lost person at the spiritual level? Because the Bible tells us they are spiritually dead (Ephesians 2:1–2; 2 Corinthians 3:12–16; 4:3–4). An unregenerate person is unable to understand or even perceive spiritual things. That is why you must often minister to a physical or soulish need in order to attract a person to address their spiritual needs.

Jesus used many different kinds of bait. One of the most successful for Him was healing. Jesus attracted people to His message of spiritual life by addressing their physical needs—namely the need to be healed from sickness and infirmity.

The Rev. Kenneth E. Hagin called healing "the dinner bell of the Gospel" because it is so often the thing that attracts a person to God. Once people get a taste of the healing part of salvation, they are going to be hungry for the whole works—spiritual, emotional, and intellectual redemption.

Another aspect of the physical realm is financial. Great financial needs can cause people to be drawn to the promises of God concerning provision and sufficiency. When people who lack financial resources find out God doesn't want them to remain poor, it can be the bait that brings them to the point of complete surrender to Christ. This is another type of physical bait.

There is soulish bait as well. A soulish bait is something that speaks to and attracts the mind, will, or emotions of a person.

A good example of this is music. Music ministers to the soulish part of man. It has enormous power to move and influence. This is precisely where much of the church world has missed it through the years.

Many folks, influenced by religious tradition, have claimed that godly music had to come out of a pipe organ or some dusty old hymnal. How many times have you heard some pious-sounding person denounce Christian rock music as being of Satan? That nonsense is not biblical.

Musical style is strictly a matter of culture and preference. It's the words and spirit behind the music that make it either glorifying to God or a tool of Satan. Different people simply like different types of music. One likes Lawrence Welk. Another likes heavy metal.

I've seen nearly every style of music utilized effectively to glorify God and draw people to Him. Music is only one among many types of soulish bait that can be used to influence others for Christ.

4. PRESENT THE BAIT CORRECTLY

As every fisherman knows, it's often not enough merely to go where the fish are hungry and use the right bait. You must also present that bait correctly to really be successful. The best presentation in fishing is one which doesn't in any way appear artificial to the fish. In other words, it's genuine.

The same is true in presenting the Gospel. Any hint of phoniness or insincerity is sure to turn a person off to the Gospel. *Compassion* is the key to your presentation.

Jesus, for example, was always moved by compassion when He ministered. We, too, need to be moved by compassion when we minister. We need to spend enough time asking God to show us His heart for the lost so that His love and compassion come across when we talk about Him to others. When you present the bait (God's willingness to meet a physical or soulish need) with that kind of compassion, you'll be perceived as sincere.

That's when it's time, as the fishermen say, to set the hook. You bring that person into a loving confrontation with Jesus Christ.

You present Him as the Way, the Truth, and the Life. But you don't stop there. There is another step.

5. REEL THEM IN

Have you ever heard of a fisherman going to all the expense and effort of hooking a fish and then just laying his rod down and walking away? Of course not. He reels the fish into the boat. It's the reason and objective of everything he's done up to that point.

When you reel in a fish, you take him out of his old environment (the water) and pull him into a new environment (the air). When lost people take the hook of life by making Jesus Christ their Lord, you then must reel them in by pulling them out of their old environment, the world, into their new environment, the body of Christ—the Church. But be warned, like some fish, new believers will often put up quite a fight. They'll strongly resist any suggestion that they get involved in a church.

That's when you have to be a skillful fisherman. If that baby Christian stays out there in the world, he'll be cut off from his source of supply and nurture. It's absolutely essential that new believers get involved in the life of a Spirit-filled, Bible-believing, Word-preaching church.

When you influence people to make a commitment to Jesus Christ, invite them to go to church with you. Offer to come pick them up. Try inviting them to other events, such as small groups, which might not be as intimidating as a full-blown worship service. Do

31

whatever you have to do to get that fish in the boat. That's the strategy of evangelism.

"Okay, Mac, I want to influence others for Jesus, but I don't know what to say." Read on. In clear terms, we'll define the message of the Gospel and help you deliver it in a way that comes as naturally as breathing in and out.

Chapter 4

FILLING THE BLACK HOLES

Black holes. In space, they are incredibly dense objects which suck in everything around them, even light. They are the ultimate, infinitely dark void.

In a sense, most people carry around a type of black hole on the inside of them. These black holes are nagging, unanswered questions and the empty, haunting sense that life has no meaning. Why is there so much suffering in the world? What is the secret of the miracle of life? What lies beyond the veil of death? Is there a God? Satan? A literal heaven and hell?

These are issues that defy the grasp of the human intellect. No matter how much education a person has, no matter how many great philosophers one reads, meaningful answers to these questions will always elude those not in the family of God. They remain black holes.

We are living in a world full of people with these black holes. Rampant drug abuse, the high suicide rate, the popularity of strange religions and the pursuit of riches all testify of man's futile quest to fill these holes apart from God. It simply can't be done. I know. I've tried, as did many of you.

King David knew a little bit about black holes. Many of his psalms express his search for answers and his occasional sense of emptiness: "The cords of death entangled me, the anguish of the grave came upon me; I was overcome by trouble and sorrow" (Psalms 116:3 NIV).

But unlike unbelievers today, David knew how to get his black holes filled: "Then I called on the name of the Lord: 'O Lord, save me!'" (v. 4).

There is only one source of light and life for mankind's black holes. A heartfelt cry to God of "HELP!" The inevitable result of such a cry is peace and rest: "Be at rest once more, O my soul, for the Lord has been good to you. For you, O Lord, have delivered my soul from death, my eyes from tears, my feet from stumbling" (vv. 7–8).

I know firsthand what it feels like to look inside and see nothing but a big gaping hole. Following two tours of duty as a pilot in Southeast Asia, I started an air freight business that rapidly grew and prospered. My wife and I had much the world says a person should ever need or want to achieve happiness. Yet, I grew more empty and miserable with each passing month.

Finally, I came to the realization that the only thing that was going to fill that black hole was Jesus. As I totally committed my life to Christ, I found the fulfillment, peace, and wholeness I had been missing for so long.

Jesus, and only Jesus, can fill your black holes. That is the simple, but profound message we must carry to those around us who are lost. It is only in entering a right relationship with Jesus that our questions get answered, life takes on meaning and the emptiness inside gets filled.

Evangelism involves leading others to a realization of a few simple truths. Here are the steps to entering a right relationship with Jesus Christ. They're the very steps you took if you know Jesus as Lord and Savior.

1. ACKNOWLEDGING SIN AND SEPARATION

Every person born into this earth enters it separated from God and spiritually dead. Why? Because our forefather, Adam, rebelled against God and we are all descended from Him.

That may be hard to comprehend on an intellectual level, but most lost people, deep down inside, are well aware of a sense of separation from God. Romans 3:23 says, "For all have sinned and fall short of the glory of God." And Romans 6:23 says, "For the wages of sin is death, but the gift of God is eternal life in Christ Jesus our Lord."

How does a person get from a state of spiritual death to a state of spiritual life and restoration? Jesus said, "You must be born again." That's a phrase that's been used and abused quite frequently. Some people equate being "born again" with something extreme or fanatical, but all it refers to is the wondrous newness of life you experience when the Spirit of God makes you spiritually alive.

The first step in this process is acknowledging your sin and recognizing a need to be restored to a relationship with God.

2. CONFESSION

The next step on the road to restoration involves confession. Specifically confessing with your mouth that Jesus Christ is Lord (boss, master, king). Romans 10:9–10 makes this very clear:

> *That if you confess with your mouth the Lord Jesus and believe in your heart that God has raised Him from the dead, you will be saved. For with the heart one believes to righteousness, and with the mouth confession is made unto salvation.*

You can't keep a real, life-changing commitment to Jesus Christ a secret. You can't say, "I'm going to make Jesus Lord of my life, but I'm not going to tell anyone about it." Jesus said if we are ashamed to confess Him before men, He can't confess us before the Father (Matthew 10:32–33).

Furthermore, the Bible tells us faith without corresponding action is dead (James 2:17). True faith in Jesus Christ will be accomplished by the action of confessing Him publicly as Lord and Savior.

These two steps, 1) acknowledgment of and repentance from sin, and 2) public confession of Jesus Christ as Lord and Savior, are the two primary acts of obedience that allow the Holy Spirit to initiate the miracle of regeneration called the new birth.

A prayer that you could lead a person in who desired to make this type of commitment might go something like this:

> *"God in Heaven, I come to You in the name of Jesus. I am sorry that I tried to fill my life with everything but You. I've*

been looking in the wrong places for answers the world can't give. But I'm glad to know I can change that.

"I have decided to believe that Jesus is Your Son. And that He died for me and rose again that I might have eternal life. I believe the black holes in my life are being filled.

"Jesus, come into my heart. Be my Savior. Be my Lord. To the best of my ability, I will live for You all of my life. This I pray in Jesus' name, amen."

Once a person makes this commitment, it is important that they grow in knowledge and relationship with God by spending time in His Word and in prayer.

SHARE THE GOOD NEWS

That, in a nutshell, is the message of the Gospel. It tells a hurting world, "You can get your black holes filled." It's as simple as that.

In another sense, the message of evangelism is a message of reconciliation. Lifestyle evangelism is simply being available to tell the people who cross your path they can be reconciled to a God who loves them.

One of the best ways to influence others with this message is through what we call "testimony." In fact, your personal testimony is the most powerful vehicle you have for communicating Jesus to other people.

In the book of Acts, Paul gives his personal testimony on three separate occasions. Each time he was evangelizing a king or governor in an attempt to persuade them to follow Christ.

"But, Mac, I don't have a very exciting testimony." I've heard many people say that. In fact, I used to say the very same thing. I'd listen to other people give testimonies about being delivered from heroin addiction or prison. Others would testify of being near the brink of death with terminal cancer when Jesus appeared to them, healed them, and they gave their lives to Him.

I'd think, "Man, compared to them, my testimony is pretty boring." Then the Lord dealt with me and said, "Your testimony is just as powerful as any other when you tell from your heart what I have done for you."

No matter who you are, if Jesus lives in your heart, you have a good testimony. All you have to do is let the Spirit of God bring it to life as you obey His prompting to share it.

Chapter 5

DISCOVERING YOUR EVANGELISM STYLE

When you hear the word "evangelist," what image springs to mind? If you're like most people you probably think of a flamboyant, outgoing, bold, brash, Bible-pounding character who never met a stranger in his life.

That's the stereotypical image of an evangelist in most believers' minds. And that's precisely why so many Christians shrink from the prospect of influencing others for Jesus. They believe they must somehow force themselves into that stereotypical mold to be an effective evangelist. Well, I have news for you. Nothing could be further from the truth.

If you can't see yourself standing on a street corner waving a Bible and shouting at passersby, relax. You don't have to become someone you're not to successfully evangelize. In fact, there is a style of evangelism that perfectly fits your temperament, personality, and gifts. It's your own unique brand of lifestyle evangelism.

Don't misunderstand. I'm not putting down aggressive, in-your-face street evangelism. There's a time and place for that. Most importantly, there are people whose personalities and gifts make them ideally suited for it. If you're one of them, more power to you. Go for it.

The fact remains, however, that many believers have no business trying to be involved in this type of evangelism on a regular basis. It's tragic that so many Christians have spent years feeling guilty, condemned, and discouraged simply because they weren't Dynamic Dave or Soapbox Sue.

The truth of the matter is, most of the lost world will never be reached through the more aggressive styles of evangelism. Most people don't respond to it. If we limit ourselves to that one type of evangelism, we're never going to reach a large percentage of this lost and hurting world.

This is why it is vital that you understand that your unique type of evangelism, whatever it may be, is just as important and needed as the stereotypical one. There is somebody in the world that needs to hear about Jesus Christ from somebody exactly like you. That fact is one of the reasons God made you like He did—He needs your style of evangelism.

If you can learn to relax and be yourself, you can develop a style of evangelism that, instead of being a burdensome chore, will become an exciting anticipated adventure.

Are you ready to discover your ideal style of evangelism? The following pages can help. But be aware that there are as many different styles of evangelism as there are personalities. We'll examine several of the most basic ones. Once you begin to direct your thinking away from the old stereotypes and toward finding out what style best suits you, finding your own style will be easy.

CONFRONTATIONAL EVANGELISM

This is the style of evangelism that best describes the old stereotype of the street preacher. This is the style that usually brings people into an abrupt confrontation with the Gospel and forces them to either accept it or reject it.

We see a good biblical example of this style being used in the context of mass evangelism in Acts 2. There, Peter and the apostles, having just been filled with the Holy Spirit, walked out onto the crowded streets of Jerusalem and started proclaiming Jesus. Peter in essence said, "Hey, listen! You killed the Son of God, but He died and rose again to save you. Accept Him as your Messiah." Three thousand people did so on the spot.

Mass evangelism is almost always confrontational, but it is equally effective in a one-on-one context. It's not surprising that Peter was involved in the above example of confrontational evangelism. It fit his personality perfectly.

The Peter we see in the Bible is a man of action. He was always the one to climb out of the boat or jump up and slice off a soldier's ear. He was also a man who didn't mince words. Clearly, diplomacy and tact were not Peter's strengths.

Many believers today flow very effectively in this type of evangelism. There is a man in my church who operates beautifully in the confrontational style of evangelism. He'll walk down the street, stop somebody, shake their hand and say, "Do you know if you're going to heaven or hell?" That's about as blunt as you can get. Yet, this style has been very effective for him. Many precious people will spend eternity in heaven because of this man's efforts.

Does that mean you have to do the same thing to please God and be effective as an evangelist? Of course not. Perhaps this next style of evangelism is more suited to your temperament.

INTELLECTUAL EVANGELISM

There are some people who will never be reached through confrontational evangelism. It does nothing but turn them off and harden them to the message of the Gospel. Some people need to be reasoned with.

Paul recognized that fact. Throughout his missionary journeys, Paul had preached a plain, simple Gospel message. But in Athens, Greece, the birthplace of ancient philosophy, he encountered a totally different type of audience. You'll find the account in Acts 17:18:

> *Then certain Epicurean and Stoic philosophers encountered him. And some said, "What does this babbler want to say?" Others said, "He seems to be a proclaimer of foreign gods," because he preached to them Jesus and the resurrection.*

When presented with an opportunity to influence a group of intellectual philosophers, Paul chose the approach of reason. He developed a brilliant argument filled with references to the Greeks' own deities and poetic writings. Some of these intellectuals rejected Paul's message, but others believed.

These men were not going to be moved by Peter's confrontational style. No, God knew that only a "Paul" could reach these men. Paul was highly educated and trained in the art of debate and logical reasoning. Paul, using the Greeks' own frame of reference, constructed a tight, well-reasoned case for accepting Jesus Christ as the risen Son of God.

This is the intellectual style of evangelism and it is perfectly suited to some Christians. More importantly, it represents the only style that is going to reach a certain segment of the population.

"But, Mac, isn't it wrong to intellectualize the Gospel?" Not at all. The truth of the Bible will stand the test of the most rigorous scrutiny. You don't have to turn your brain off when you accept Jesus Christ. On the contrary, giving one's life to Christ is the most logical, reasonable thing a person can do.

If this style of evangelism is attractive to you, start developing it. Then listen for the Holy Spirit's promptings to use it. He'll direct you to the people who need to hear it.

RELATIONAL EVANGELISM

This, in a nutshell, involves evangelism with your family and friends. You might be thinking, "Anybody can do that." On the contrary, many Christians are totally ineffective in evangelizing the people they love.

For any number of reasons, certain believers simply alienate everyone close to them immediately after being born again. The relational evangelist, on the other hand, is specially gifted at bringing friends and loved ones into the kingdom. They're comfortable with it. They want to do it. And they're effective at it.

Jesus drove a legion of demons out of a tormented man and then commissioned him and sent him forth as this very type of evangelist.

As Jesus was getting into the boat, the man who had been demon-possessed begged to go with him. Jesus did not let him, but said, "Go home to your family and tell them how much the Lord has done for you, and how he has had mercy on you." So the man went away and began to tell in the Decapolis how much Jesus had done for him. And all the people were amazed. (Mark 5:18–20 NIV)

If you're this type of evangelist, don't minimize your contribution to the plans and purposes of God. I remember counseling with a man who was suffering under a huge load of condemnation. He felt he was a failure as an evangelist. As it turned out, in the preceding two years he had systematically won his father, mother, sisters, brothers, and six friends to Jesus. That's not failure. But because he didn't fit the mold of the confrontational evangelist, he felt it was.

Relational evangelism is a very valid and needed style of evangelism. If it feels right for you, move and grow in it. Simply consider your circle of relatives and friends as your own personal missions field.

SERVICE EVANGELISM

In Acts 9, we're introduced to a remarkable woman named Tabitha. She typifies yet another style of effective evangelism—service evangelism.

At Joppa there was a certain disciple named Tabitha, which is translated Dorcas. This woman was full of good works and charitable deeds which she did. But it happened in those days that she became sick and died. When they had washed her, they laid her in an upper room. And since Lydda was near Joppa, and the disciples had heard that Peter was there, they sent two men to him, imploring him not to delay in coming to them. Then Peter arose and went with them. When he had come, they brought him to the upper room. And all the widows stood by him weeping, showing the tunics and garments which Dorcas had made while she was with them. (Acts 9:36–39)

Here's a woman who testified to her entire community, not with words but with good deeds. This represents a powerful style of evangelism that is frequently overlooked.

If you're not comfortable with the prospect of looking for an opening to verbally influence someone for Jesus, you can still reach them by finding some way to serve them in a meaningful way. Then, when they ask how they can thank you, simply say, "How about going to church with me this Sunday?" Being a servant opens the door to an invitation.

I know a pastor whose church experienced phenomenal growth, primarily through service evangelism. He had started his church in a northern city with just a handful of people. They had scraped together enough money to buy a little truck with a snowplow on the front in order to keep the parking lot clear on snowy days.

After the next heavy snow, at the prompting of the Spirit, this pastor got up before dawn and cleared the driveways of all the homes around the church. Imagine the astonishment and gratitude when people awoke to find their driveway clear and a church business card in the door which read, "Courtesy of the church that cares for you. We wanted to do this for you."

Many of those families ended up going to that pastor's church and being saved. The church grew from three families to 300 people in the first 18 months.

Service evangelism is a powerful thing. Never feel condemned if this is your preferred style of evangelism. It's valid. It's effective. And it's biblical.

INVITATIONAL EVANGELISM

Remember the biblical account of Jesus and the Samaritan woman at the well in John 4? After a life-changing experience with Jesus Christ, this woman practiced another important style of evangelism. We see it beginning in verse 28:

The woman then left her waterpot, went her way into the city, and said to the men, "Come, see a Man who told me all things that I ever did. Could this be the Christ?" Then they went out of the city and came to Him. (John 4:28–30)

The essence of the message of the invitational evangelist consists of two simple words. They are, "Come see." You don't have to be a bold confrontationist. You don't have to be an intellectual persuader. To be an effective evangelist, all you need is the willingness to say, "Come and listen to what this man has to say." The results this woman received speak for themselves.

And many of the Samaritans of that city believed in Him because of the word of the woman who testified, "He told me all that I ever did." So when the Samaritans had come to Him, they urged Him to stay with them; and He stayed there two days. And many more believed because of His own word. (John 4:39–41)

"Just invite them to a meeting, Mac? Isn't that a cop-out?"

Some people may think so, but nothing could be further from the truth. This woman was used to bring a whole city to Jesus. I call that highly effective evangelism. Yet it didn't take a polished orator or a fearless street preacher. It merely took someone who cared enough to issue an invitation.

If you're not comfortable with any of the other types of evangelism we've discussed thus far, you may want to try this style. It's not a cop-out. It's not a compromise. It's another valid method which is just right for some people's personalities.

FINDING YOUR NICHE

There are many other styles of evangelism I haven't mentioned here. In fact, I believe there are as many different styles of evangelism as there are personality types.

Some people are children's evangelists. They are most effective and gratified when ministering the Gospel to children. Others are cultural evangelists. These are people who are ideally suited for ministering to a narrow segment of our society. The list is endless.

The key to finding your special niche in influencing others with the Gospel is to first break out of the old ways of thinking about it. Shatter your stereotypical mental images of what an evangelist looks and acts like. Then start seeing yourself as a unique and specially gifted evangelist. Get up every morning and say, "I am a fisher of men."

As you begin to recognize and develop your own style of evangelism, you'll discover an excitement unequaled by anything else in the Christian life. I've found that using the God-given gifts that are uniquely mine to bring others to Jesus Christ is the most exhilarating experience I've ever known. It makes flying a high performance jet at twice the speed of sound seem downright boring by comparison.

Remember, there are people out there who aren't going to receive the Gospel from anyone but you. If you'll stay sensitive to the Spirit and ready to be used, you'll find them. Once you've discovered your best method of lifestyle evangelism, winning them will come as naturally as walking.

As an added benefit, you'll begin to experience the power of God in your life in ways you never dreamed. It's the power that is released as you align yourself with God's great plan to bring a fallen world back into relationship with Him. It's the power experienced only by those who dare to influence others for Jesus.

PRAYER OF SALVATION

God wants everyone to receive eternal salvation. The way to receive this salvation is to call upon the name of Jesus and confess Him as your Lord. The Bible says, "That if thou shalt confess with thy mouth the Lord Jesus, and shalt believe in thine heart that God hath raised him from the dead, thou shalt be saved. ... For whosoever shall call upon the name of the Lord shall be saved" (Romans 10:9, 13).

Jesus has given salvation, healing, and countless benefits to all who call upon His name. These benefits can be yours if you receive Him into your heart by praying this prayer:

Heavenly Father, I come to You admitting that I am a sinner. Right now, I choose to turn away from sin, and I ask You to cleanse me of all unrighteousness. I believe that Your Son, Jesus, died on the cross to take away my sins. I also believe that He rose again from the dead so that I may be justified and made righteous through faith in Him. I call upon the name of Jesus Christ to be the Savior and Lord of my life. Jesus, I choose to follow You, and I ask that You fill me with the power of the Holy Spirit. I declare right now that I am a born again child of God. I am free from sin and full of the righteousness of God. I am saved in Jesus' name, amen.

If you have just received Jesus Christ as your Savior, or if this book has changed your life, we would like to hear from you. Please call us at 763.315.7200 or email us at info@mac-hammond.org.

ABOUT THE AUTHOR

Mac Hammond is senior pastor of Living Word Christian Center, a large and growing church in Brooklyn Park (a suburb of Minneapolis), Minnesota. He is the host of the Winner's Way broadcast and author of several internationally distributed books. Mac is broadly acclaimed for his ability to apply the principles of the Bible to practical situations and the challenges of daily living.

Mac Hammond graduated from Virginia Military Institute in 1965. Upon graduation, he entered the Air Force and received his wings in November 1966. He subsequently served two tours of duty in Southeast Asia, accumulating 198 combat missions. He was honorably discharged in 1970 with the rank of Captain.

Between 1970 and 1980, Mac was involved in varying capacities in the general aviation industry including ownership of a successful air cargo business serving the Midwestern United States. A business acquisition brought the Hammonds to Minneapolis where they ultimately founded Living Word Christian Center in 1980 with 12 people in attendance.

After 38 years, that group of twelve people has grown into an active church body of more than 10,000 members. Today some of the outreaches that spring from Living Word include Maranatha Christian Academy, Living Free Recovery Services, The Wells at 7th Street, CFAITH, and a national and international media outreach that includes hundreds of audio/video teaching series, a half-hour television broadcast called *The Winner's Way* with Mac Hammond, seen nationwide, and a daily 60-second television commentary called the *Winner's Minute.*

Mac Hammond Ministries
PO Box 29469
Minneapolis, Minnesota 55429-2946

You can also visit us on the web at
machammond.org.

OTHER BOOKS BY MAC HAMMOND

Angels at Your Service
Releasing the Power of Heaven's Host

The Big Picture
Living Your Life in Light of Eternity

Doorways to Deception
How Deception Comes, How It Destroys, and How You Can Avoid It

Following the Fire
Discovering How God Leads You by the Desires of Your Heart

Heirs Together
Solving the Mystery of a Satisfying Marriage

The Last Millennium
A Revealing Look at the Remarkable Days Ahead
and How You Can Live Them to the Fullest

Living Safely in a Dangerous World
Keys to Abiding in the Secret Place

Plugged In and Prospering
How to Find and Fill Your God-Ordained Place in the Local Church

Positioned for Promotion
How to Increase Your Influence and Capacity to Lead

Real Faith Never Fails
Detecting (and Correcting) Four Common Faith Mistakes

Simplifying Your Life
Divine Insights to Uncomplicated Living

Soul Control
Whoever Controls Your Soul, Controls Your Destiny

The Suffering Question
Biblical Insights Into Why Bad Things Happen to Good People

Water, Wind, & Fire
Understanding the New Birth and the Baptism of the Holy Spirit

Water, Wind, & Fire—The Next Steps
Developing Your New Relationship With God

The Way of the Winner
Running the Race to Victory

Who God Is Not
Exploding the Myths About His Nature and His Ways

Winning In Your Finances
How to Walk God's Pathway to Prosperity

Yielded and Bold
How to Understand and Flow With the Move of God's Spirit

For a complete list of available resources,
please visit us on the web at **machammond.org**
or you may also contact us at:

Mac Hammond Ministries
PO Box 29469
Minneapolis, Minnesota 55429-2946